AF230884

First Published 2023 by Snowdrop Publishing
www.Snowdrop-Publishing.com

ISBN: 978-1-916703-00-1

A CIP catalogue record for this book is available from the British Library

Notes to Parents and Carers

This book has been designed as a tool to help parents and carers open up a dialogue about self-protection and keeping ourselves safe in childhood and beyond. My hope is that if a similar situation occurred where a child felt uneasy, or perhaps they had a friend who they were worried about, they will have learned from this book that they can speak to someone straight away, no matter how big or small the problem seems.

We need to arm our children with the knowledge to protect themselves - because we can't be there all the time.

Remember knowledge is power, and forewarned is forearmed. Let's work together to arm the next generation of children

Guidance for reading Laura's Secret'

Explain to your child(ren) that you are going to read a story and it would be wonderful if they could listen well. Allow them to look carefully at the cover of the book.

Read the title and ask,

- What is a secret?

Note: We suggest you don't go into 'good' and 'bad' secrets or surprises at this stage, as this will come up through the discussion questions at the back of the book.

- Who do you think the little girl is?
- How do you think the little girl is feeling?
- Why do you think she is feeling this way?

Read the story through the first time round, so that the storyline is not lost. Once the story is finished, go to the discussion questions with the child(ren). Spend as long as appropriate on each question.

Note: When reading the story again, it is important to stop to discuss the illustrations when appropriate, discuss the little girl's body language with your child and ask them how Laura might be feeling.

Revisit the story a few days or a week later.

Ask Your child

- Do you remember this story?
- What was it about?
- What happened to the little girl?
- Should we keep secrets such as someone touching our private parts?
- Was the little girl right to tell someone about what happened to her?
- What would you do if someone touched your private parts?

Reinforce that the child must tell the person touching them to "Stop," and they must tell someone they trust straight away, and keep on telling until they are helped.

Discuss briefly when it is appropriate for someone else to touch their body, e.g. a doctor, or nurse, but explain that it's only if a parent or trusted adult is in the room with them.

Continuing on from this discussion, have children share who they would tell if they are feeling unsafe or experiencing early warning signs.
Discuss how this person is someone they can talk to about anything. It is a person who always listens to them and someone they can contact or find easily.

When appropriate, read the story again and revisit protective behaviours.

Further resources on this topic:

https://www.parentsprotect.co.uk/

https://www.nspcc.org.uk/

Ask your child to find the butterfly on each page of the story 

Body Safety

Body Safety Education (also known as protective behaviours or child sexual abuse prevention education) involves so much more than focusing on stranger danger. In fact, 95% of sexually abused children will know their abuser and only 5% will be strangers.

It is also crucial for children to learn that they must never keep secrets that make them feel bad or uncomfortable (in fact, we teach it's best not to have secrets in families, only happy surprises). The trouble with secrets is that they are the main tool used by child molesters to ensure children remain silent about the abuse. Ensuring the secret is kept is of utmost importance to the perpetrator. Therefore, threats and insisting no one will believe the child is used as a way of controlling the child to be silent.

Through Body Safety Education parents and children will learn the importance of there being no secrets between us. Parents and carers need to be on the lookout for signs of sexual abuse in children and grooming behaviour which is often focused on themselves as well as their children.

The answer to the question, 'How do I keep kids safe from sexual abuse?' is simple; teach them Body Safety Education from a very young age. Always use the correct names for their genitals, ensure they know that the parts covered by their swimsuit are known as their private parts, and that private means 'just for you', and consequently not for sharing. This is known as the swimsuit lesson.

When you teach your child that 'your body belongs to you' you are empowering them with confidence through knowledge. Body Safety Education also involves teaching your child that no one can touch their private parts, and if they do, they must tell a trusted adult until believed.

Kids need to be safe as well as feel safe. Teaching a child that private means 'just for you' and that their private parts are found under their swimsuit is a valuable lesson that can prevent child molestation.

Approximately 1 in 3 girls and 1 in 6 boys will be sexually abused before their 18th birthday. You can help stop child abuse by teaching social and physical boundaries to kids and that some parts are not for sharing.

Laura's Secret

Laura was a little girl who lived in a busy, happy house with her mum, dad, brother, two sisters, and their two dogs. Laura always did as she was told.

She loved going to school and playing with her
friends. Laura enjoyed singing and dancing.

She was always trying to please people and didn't like it when other people were sad or upset - especially if she thought they were sad or upset because of her.

But then her family began
to change. Laura and her
brother and sisters went
to live in a new house
with Mum.

A new man moved in with them.
Soon after, he married Mum and
became their stepdad.

Something about Laura's stepdad made her feel uncomfortable. Sometimes he seemed nice, but other times he was mean to her and scary. He made her do things she didn't like, things she didn't understand.

Laura didn't like it when her stepdad hugged her. It was different from Mum's hugs. She never felt safe when he was around. She didn't like it when he tickled her, or when he kissed her when no one was looking. Everything felt strange and wrong, and Laura didn't know why.

She didn't know the words to explain what was happening, or why she didn't like it. Her stepdad made her promise that she would never tell. She wanted to scream or run away but each time she tried she was frozen and nothing came out. Laura didn't like having secrets from Mum, it made her feel very confused.

Laura would cry every night before she went to sleep, she was always worrying about the secret.

Even in the daytime, she would be sad and worried.

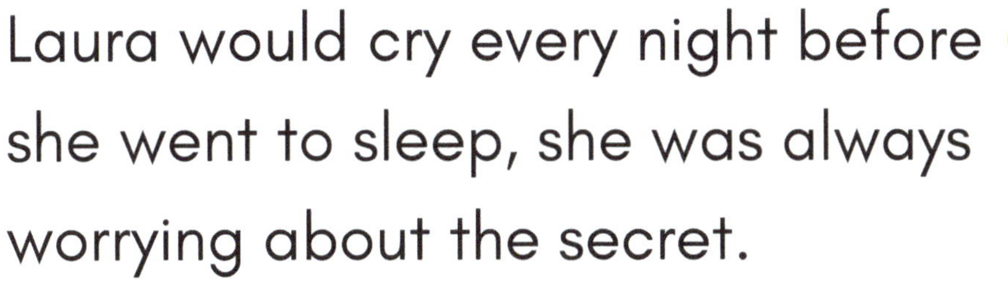

Her stepdad told her that Mum wouldn't love her anymore if Laura told her, or anyone else, about the secret.

Laura began to get sick. No one understood why.
Laura didn't know why either. She just wanted to
disappear. A long time passed, and Laura
wanted to give up.

One day, Laura realised what she had to do – she had to tell the secret. She had to be brave. She told the person she trusted most in the whole world– who told her she was right to tell, she was very brave and promised Laura that her stepdad would never, ever, hurt her again.

At last, Laura felt she could breathe once again.

Then Laura told someone else, and again she felt
better. The more people she told her secret to, the
smaller it became and the more she started to
understand it.

Laura didn't have to run away, she wasn't in trouble,
and she had done nothing wrong, she knew that now.

Now Laura knows that some secrets should never be kept and that if something feels wrong, you should talk about it with someone you trust to help you make things right again.

Laura wished she had talked to someone straight away, so she didn't have to spend so long feeling poorly and sad, and now she spreads her message to other boys and girls like you, to make sure you know what to do if you ever have a secret you don't want to keep.

Did your child find a butterfly on every page?
Butterflies are a symbol of hope.

Questions to ask your child after reading Laura's Secret

- Which of the children on the opposite page do you think would be most likely to have a secret like Laura's? Then explain to your child(ren) that anyone can be abused - girls and boys from all over the world, it doesn't matter if you are rich or poor, everyone needs to be able to protect themselves.
- Why didn't Laura tell someone straight away about the secret?
- Should she have?
- Should anyone touch your private parts?
- If they do, what should you do?

Talk about trusted adults - and how this can change depending on the situation.

- Who would you tell if you had a secret you didn't want to keep?

Discuss the difference between 'good' and 'bad' secrets.

Good Secrets

- Make you feel happy.
- Are about happy things.
- Never scare you.

Bad Secrets

- Make you feel sad or sick.
- Are about breaking the rules.
- Scare you.

Check if your child(ren) has any further questions, remember there are lots of resources online on the Parent Protect website, www.parentsprotect.co.uk, or via the NSPCC, www.nspcc.org.uk

What should you do if a child comes to you and tells you that they are being abused?

- Remain Calm
- Receive: Listen to what is being said without displaying shock or disbelief. Accept what is being said without judgement. Take it seriously.
- Reassure: Reassure the child, but only so far as is honest and reliable. Don't make promises that you can't be sure to keep, e.g. "everything will be all right now". Reassure the child that they did nothing wrong and that you take what is said seriously. Don't promise confidentiality - never agree to keep secrets. You have a duty to report your concerns. Tell the child that you will need to tell some people, but only those whose job it is to protect children. Acknowledge how difficult it must have been to talk. It takes a lot for a child to come forward about abuse.
- React: Listen quietly, carefully and patiently. Do not assume anything - don't speculate or jump to conclusions. Do not investigate, interrogate or decide if the child is telling the truth. Let the child explain to you in his or her own words what happened, but don't ask leading questions. Do ask open questions like "Is there anything else that you want to tell me?" Communicate with the child in a way that is appropriate to their age, understanding and preference.
- Record: Make some very brief notes at the time and write them up in detail as soon as possible.
- Contact Childline for advice on what to do next

Dedicated to anyone who has ever been,
or still is, deafened by the silence.

About the Author

Laura lives with her family in Northumberland. She sings and teaches singing professionally and is passionate about raising awareness and preventing any child from having to go through a situation like hers alone. You can contact Laura via Instagram @laurassecretbook

www.ingramcontent.com/pod-product-compliance
Lightning Source LLC
Chambersburg PA
CBHW042158030726
47599CB00004B/786